*I am delighted to recommend
this booklet and the entire
RZIM Critical Questions Series
to you. Written in a popular style and
engaging manner, these booklets are
authored by many notable thinkers and
respected scholars.*

*They are uniquely and specifically
designed for those who have
questions about—and even
difficulties with—belief in God and the
credibility of the Christian faith.*

*Christian believers, too, will greatly
benefit from this series, which will serve
as an important tool to present and
defend their faith in the
marketplace of ideas.*

*I am convinced that these
remarkable booklets will not
disappoint in their readability and in
their persuasiveness for those honestly
seeking answers to life's deepest questions
and to the cultural
confusion around us.*

Ravi K. Zacharias

1

GOD, ARE YOU THERE?

Five Reasons God Exists and Three Reasons It Makes a Difference

William Lane Craig

has a Ph.D. in philosophy from the University of Birmingham and a D.Theol. from the University of Munich. He is a noted lecturer and debater and has written numerous articles for such prominent journals as the *Journal of Philosophy, Philosophy, Philosophical Studies, British Journal for the Philosophy of Science, Australasian Journal of Philosophy, International Studies in the Philosophy of Science*, and *New Testament Studies*. His books include *The Cosmological Argument from Plato to Leibniz* (Macmillan), *The Son Rises* (Moody Press), *Divine Foreknowledge and Human Freedom* (E.J. Brill), *The Only Wise God* (Baker), (co-authored) *Theism, Atheism, and Big Bang Cosmology* (Clarendon Press), and *Reasonable Faith* (Crossway Books). He is research professor of philosophy at Talbot School of Theology and is an adjunct lecturer for Ravi Zacharias International Ministries in Norcross, Georgia. He resides in Atlanta with his wife Jan and their two children, Charity and John.

ISBN 1-930107-00-5

GOD, ARE YOU THERE?

Five Reasons God Exists and Three Reasons It Makes a Difference

William Lane Craig

Introduction

Western philosophy, observes James Collins, has carried the burden of God.[1] From the first glimmerings of philosophy among the ancient Greeks up through the dawn of the third millennium after Christ, the world's greatest thinkers from Plato to Plantinga have wrestled with the question of God. Is there a personal, transcendent being who created the universe and is the source of moral goodness?

Unfortunately, as our universities have increasingly departed from the classical, liberal arts curriculum, students typically find themselves ill-informed and poorly trained to deal with this issue. Rather than reflect rationally on the question, students far too often merely absorb uncritically the easy answers and secular prejudices of their teachers. A professional colleague describes the situation all too well:

> As a teacher of "critical thinking, writing, and reading" in the Rhetoric and Writing Department at _____, I've read thousands of student papers relating to life origins, personal philosophy/relativism, and the like. The overwhelming majority of students relate stories of mind-expanding courses which taught them to think 'critically' (i.e., to reject God or conventional morality) and which are responsible for their agnosticism/atheism. The funny thing is that the stories are all alike, and when pressed further, very few students have reasons for their new-found faith in . . . well, nothing. They have simply trusted

that charismatic biology/anthropology/ philoso-phy/political science prof. who 'disproved' the existence of God using arguments as pathetic as "It's obvious . . . ."[2]

My own experience in talking with students is that most of them are incapable of clearly articulating reasons for their views about God. This goes not only for unbelievers, but also for believing students, who often seem to be incapable of giving any reason for their religious faith.

THREE REASONS IT MAKES A DIFFERENCE

Perhaps part of the reason for people's lack of ability to articulate clear reasons for their views about God is that people generally think that it really doesn't make any difference what you believe about God, whether God exists or does not exist. But people who shrug their shoulders and say, "What difference does it make whether God exists or not?" simply reveal that they haven't thought very deeply about this question. Even atheist philosophers like Jean Paul Sartre and Albert Camus—who did think deeply about this question—recognized that the existence of God makes a tremendous difference to man. Let's consider just three reasons why it makes a big difference whether God exists.

1. *If God does not exist, then life is ultimately meaningless.* If your life is doomed to end in death, then ultimately it does not matter how you live. In the end it makes no ultimate difference whether you existed or not. Sure, your life might have a *relative* significance in that you influenced others or affected the course of history. But ultimately mankind is doomed to perish in the heat death of the universe. Ultimately it makes no difference who you are or what you do. Your life is inconsequential.

Certainly we can try to create meaning for our lives by inventing certain projects and purposes to occupy ourselves until our deaths. This will supply a *subjective* sense of meaning to our lives (indeed, without such a subjective sense it is doubtful that life would be bearable). But ultimately these projects and purposes themselves make no difference and so cannot be a source of ultimate significance for us. There is no *objective* purpose to our lives, and ultimately it makes no difference whether our petty projects are fulfilled or not. They supply us with an illusion of significance and meaning, but like shuffling deck chairs on the Titanic, they are inconsequential in light of our fate.

Thus, the contributions of the scientist to the advancement of human knowledge, the research of the doctor to alleviate pain and suffering, the efforts of the diplomat to secure peace in the world, the sacrifices of good people everywhere to better the lot of the human race—ultimately all these come to nothing. Thus, if atheism is true, life is ultimately meaningless.

2. *If God does not exist, then we must ultimately live without hope.* If there is no God, then there is ultimately no hope for deliverance from the shortcomings of our finite existence.

For example, there is no hope for deliverance from evil. Although many people ask how God could create a world involving so much evil, by far most of the suffering in the world is due to man's own inhumanity to man. The horror of two World Wars effectively destroyed the 19th century's naive optimism about human progress. If God does not exist, then we are locked without hope in a world filled with gratuitous and unredeemed suffering, and there is no hope for deliverance from evil.

Or again, if there is no God, there is no hope of deliverance from aging, disease, and death. Although it may be hard to contemplate, the sober fact is that unless you die young, someday you—you yourself—will be an old man or an old woman, fighting a losing battle with aging, struggling against the inevitable advance of deterioration, disease, perhaps senility. And finally and inevitably you will die. There is no afterlife beyond the grave. Atheism is thus a philosophy without hope.

The atheist philosopher Bertrand Russell eloquently expressed the hopelessness and despair which inevitably attend atheism:

> That Man is the product of causes which had no prevision of the end they were achieving; that his origin, his growth, his hopes and fears, are but the outcome of accidental collocations of atoms; that all the labours of the ages, all the devotion, all the inspiration, all the noonday brightness of human genius, are destined to extinction in the vast death of the solar system, and that the whole temple of Man's achievement must inevitably be buried beneath the debris of a universe in ruins—all these things, are so nearly certain, that no philosophy which rejects them can hope to stand. Only within the scaffolding of these truths, only on the firm foundation of unyielding despair, can the soul's habitation henceforth be safely built.[3]

3. On the other hand, *if God does exist, then not only does life have meaning and hope, but there is also the possibility of coming to know God and his love personally.* Think of it! That the infinite God should love you and want to be your personal friend! It's almost too wonderful for words. Clearly, this would be the most exalted state that a human being could enjoy. Thus, if God exists, it makes not only a tremendous difference for mankind in general, but it could make a life-changing difference for you as well.

Now admittedly none of this shows that God exists. But it does show that it makes a tremendous *difference* whether God exists. And, of course, if we have been made by God to know him, then it's hardly surprising that we would have a longing for meaning and purpose in our lives. Therefore, I'm inclined to agree with the French mathematical genius Blaise Pascal that even if the evidence for and against the existence of God were absolutely equal, the rational thing to do would be to believe that God exists. That is to say, if the evidence is equal, then it seems positively irrational to prefer death, despair, and meaning-lessness to life, hope, and significance. Therefore, I'm inclined to speak of *the presumption of theism*: we ought to presume that God exists unless we have some good reason to think that atheism is true.

FIVE REASONS GOD EXISTS

Arguments for the Existence of God

But in fact I don't think that the scales of the evidence are equally balanced; I think that there are good reasons which tip the scales in favor of God's existence. In what follows I'll share with you five of those reasons.

Before I do, however, some preliminary words are important. When I speak of "reasons" for God's existence, I'm talking about arguments for the existence of God. An argument is a set of statements which serve as premises leading to a conclusion. Arguments can be either deductive or inductive. A deductive argument guarantees that the conclusion is true if the premises are true. An inductive argument makes it probable that the conclusion is true if the premises are true. I'll use both kinds of arguments below.

What makes for a good argument? Three crucial elements are involved.

First of all, *it must be sound*, which means that its premises must be true and the conclusion must follow from the premises in accord with the rules of logic.

Second, *it must not be question-begging*; that is to say, the reasons you believe the premises to be true must be independent of the argument's conclusion. Otherwise you could reason, "Either God exists or I'm a monkey's uncle; I am not a monkey's uncle; therefore, God exists." This may be a sound argument (it has true premises and follows the rules of logic), but it begs the question, since the only reason you would believe the first premise is that you already believe the conclusion.

Finally, *the premises of the argument must be more plausible than their denials*. For an argument to be a good one, it isn't required that we have 100% certainty of the truth of the premises. Some of the premises in a good argument may strike you as only slightly more plausible than their denials; other premises may seem to you highly plausible. But so long as a statement is more plausible than its negation, then you should believe it rather than its negation, and so it may serve as a premise in a good argument. Thus, a good argument for God's existence need not make it *certain* that God exists. Certainty is what most people are thinking of when they say, "You can't prove that God exists!" If we equate "proof" with 100% certainty, then we may agree with them and yet insist that there are still good reasons or good arguments to think that God exists. Thus, if someone objects to a premise in our argument by saying, "But it's possible that . . ." and state some alternative, we may happily agree. Possibilities come cheap. The question is not whether the denial of a particular premise in the argument is possible (or even plausible); the question is whether the denial is as plausible or more plausible than the premise. If it isn't, then we should believe the premise.

Now plausibility is to a great extent a person-dependent notion. Some people may find a premise plausible and others not. Accordingly, some people will agree that a particular argument is a good one, while others will say that it's a bad argument. Given our diverse backgrounds and biases, we should expect such disagreements. In cases of disagreement we have to dig deeper and ask what reasons we each have for thinking a premise to be true or false. When we do so, we may discover that it is we who have made the mistake. After all, you can present bad arguments for a true conclusion! But we might find instead that the person we're talking to has no good reason for rejecting our premise or that his rejection is based on misinformation, or ignorance of the evidence, or a fallacious objection. In such a case we may persuade him by giving him better information or evidence or by gently correcting his error. On the other hand, we may find that the reason he denies our premise is that he doesn't like the conclusion it's leading to, and so to avoid that conclusion he denies a premise which he really ought to find quite plausible.

This serves to highlight an important feature of

arguments for the existence of God. The question of God's existence has such personal significance that issues of the heart take on a paramount importance. I'm reminded in this connection of a distinction drawn by the British theologian J. I. Packer between two sorts of people with an interest in God.[4] Some people are like travelers proceeding down a hot, dusty road; others are like the people sitting on the balconies of the houses lining the road. Both the travelers and the balconeers have an interest in the road and the journey along it, and they can discuss with one another where the road leads, how difficult the journey is, and so on. Nevertheless, there remains this profound difference between the travelers and the balconeers: the travelers are actually on the road, taking the journey whereas the balconeers' interest in the road and the journey is purely theoretical—they aren't going anywhere!

In the same way I find that a person with a traveler's interest in the existence of God will approach the arguments for God's existence with a much different attitude than will a balconeer. Someone who is truly searching to find God will be open to God's existence in a way that many balconeers will not. He will approach the subject with a deep humility and be eager to find evidences of God's being. Like someone searching for a lost loved one, any trace of God's existence will excite him and inspire hope. This is not to say that he becomes gullible; but it is to say that his approach to God will involve a desire for God and an openness to finding him.

By contrast balconeers are often indifferent or even hostile to God. Here, for example, is what the philosopher Thomas Nagel has to say:

> *I want atheism to be true* and am made uneasy by the fact that some of the most intelligent and well-informed people I know are religious believers. It isn't just that I don't believe in God and, naturally, hope that I'm right in my belief. It's that *I hope there is no God! I don't want there to be a God; I don't want a universe like that.*[5]

Such a person will obviously approach the arguments for God's existence with a totally different attitude than a traveler. Rather than looking for God, he will be looking for loopholes. Rather than accept the argument's conclusion, he will deny one of its premises, no matter how implausible such a denial may seem. Every one of us has a skeptical dial which we can conveniently turn up when considering arguments for conclusions we don't like but turn down low when it comes to our own philosophy and beliefs. The hypocrisy of many balconeers is that when it comes to arguments for God's existence, they dial up their skepticism to a degree which they would never contemplate in their ordinary, everyday lives. If some people were as skeptical about everyday affairs as they are about arguments for God's existence, they would scarcely be able to function. I'm astonished, for example, at the number of atheists who, when confronted with the evidence for the origin of the universe, will say that the universe just popped into being uncaused out of nothing. Would they ever accept such an explanation in any other domain of life, say, for why the missing $10,000 was found in the bank manager's briefcase? Did it just pop into existence there? For balconeers, arguments for God's existence are at best intellectual games. They don't really expect or hope to find God at the end.

If God exists, then we really can't play intellectual games with him. Rather we must approach him with openness, reverence, and humility. If we are travelers, we shall approach the arguments for God sympathetically, rather than skeptically. Thus, the so-called "skeptical inquirer" is not really an inquirer at all. He wants *not* to believe. As we consider, then, the arguments which I'm about to share, it's important that we do so with an open mind and an open heart.

As travelers along life's way, it's our goal to make sense of things, to try to understand the way the world is. The hypothesis that God exists makes sense out of a wide range of the facts of experience.

FIRST REASON

God makes sense of the origin of the universe.

Have you ever asked yourself where the universe came from or why everything exists instead of just nothing? Typically atheists have said that the universe is just eternal, and that's all. But surely this is unreasonable. Just think about it a minute. If the universe never had a beginning, that means that the number of past events in the history of the universe is infinite. But mathematicians recognize that the idea of an actually infinite number of things leads to self-contradictions. For example, what is infinity minus infinity? Well, mathematically, you get self-contradictory answers. For example, if you subtract all the odd numbers {1, 3, 5, . . .} from all the natural numbers {0, 1, 2, 3, . . .}, how many numbers do you have left? An infinite number. So infinity minus infinity is infinity. But suppose instead you subtract all the numbers greater than 2—how many are left? Three. So infinity minus infinity is 3! It needs to be understood that in both these cases we have subtracted identical quantities from identical quantities and come up with self-contradictory answers. In fact, *you can get any answer you want* from zero to infinity! This shows that infinity is just an idea in your mind, not something that exists in reality.

David Hilbert, perhaps the greatest mathematician of this century, states, "The infinite is nowhere to be found in reality. It neither exists in nature nor provides a legitimate basis for rational thought. The role that remains for the infinite to play is solely that of an idea."[6] Therefore, since past events are not just ideas, but are real, the number of past events must be finite. Therefore, the series of past events can't go back forever; rather the universe must have begun to exist.

This conclusion has been confirmed by remarkable discoveries in astronomy and astrophysics. The astrophysical evidence indicates that the universe began to exist in a great explosion called the "Big Bang" around 15 billion years ago. Physical space and time were created in that event, as well as all the matter and energy in the universe. Therefore, as Cambridge astronomer Fred Hoyle points out, the Big Bang theory requires the creation of the universe from nothing. This is because, as one goes back in time, one reaches a point at which, in Hoyle's words, the universe was "shrunk down to nothing at all."[7] Thus, what the Big Bang model requires is that the universe began to exist and was created out of nothing.

Now this tends to be very awkward for the atheist. For as Anthony Kenny of Oxford University urges, "A proponent of the big bang theory, at least if he is an atheist, must believe that the . . . universe came from nothing and by nothing."[8] But surely that doesn't make sense! Out of nothing, nothing comes. In every other context atheists recognize this fact. The great skeptic David Hume wrote, "But allow me to tell you that I never asserted so absurd a Proposition as that *anything might arise without a cause*."[9] The contemporary atheist philosopher Kai Nielsen gives this illustration: "Suppose you suddenly hear a loud bang . . . and you ask me, 'What made that bang?' and I reply, 'Nothing, it just happened.' You would not accept that. In fact you would find my reply quite unintelligible."[10] But what's true of the little bang must be true of the Big Bang as well! So why does the universe exist instead of just nothing? Where did it come from? There must have been a cause which brought the universe into being. As the great scientist Sir Arthur Eddington said, "The beginning seems to present insuperable difficulties unless we agree to look on it as frankly supernatural."[11]

We can summarize our argument thus far as follows:

1. Whatever begins to exist has a cause.
2. The universe began to exist.
3. Therefore, the universe has a cause.

Given the truth of the two premises, the conclusion necessarily follows.

Now from the very nature of the case, as the cause of space and time, this supernatural cause must be an uncaused, changeless, timeless, and immaterial being which created the universe. It must be uncaused because we've seen that there cannot be an infinite regress of causes. It must be timeless and therefore changeless—at least without the universe—because it created time. Because it also created space, it must transcend space as well and therefore be immaterial, not physical.

Moreover, I would argue, it must also be personal. For how else could a timeless cause give rise to a temporal effect like the universe? If the cause were a mechanically operating set of necessary and sufficient conditions, then the cause could never exist without the effect. For example, the cause of water's freezing is the temperature's being below 0° Centigrade. If the temperature were below 0° from eternity past, then any water that was around would be frozen from eternity. It would be impossible for the water to *begin* to freeze just a finite time ago. So if the cause is timelessly present, then the effect should be timelessly present as well. The only way for the cause to be timeless and the effect to begin in time is for the cause to be a personal agent who freely chooses to create an effect in time without any prior determining conditions. For example, a man sitting from eternity could freely will to stand up. Thus, we are brought, not merely to a transcendent cause of the universe, but to its personal creator.

What objections might be raised against this argument? Premise (1) **Whatever begins to exist has a cause** seems obviously true—at the least, more so than its denial. Yet a number of atheists, in order to avoid the argument's conclusion, have denied the first premise. Sometimes it is said that sub-atomic physics furnishes an exception to premise (1), since on the sub-atomic level events are said to be uncaused. In the same way, certain theories of cosmic origins are interpreted as showing that the whole universe could have sprung into being out of the sub-atomic vacuum. Thus the universe is said to be the proverbial "free lunch."

This objection, however, is based on misunderstandings. In the first place, not all scientists agree that sub-atomic events are uncaused. A great many physicists today are quite dissatisfied with this view (the so-called Copenhagen Interpretation) of subatomic physics and are exploring deterministic theories like that of David Bohm.[12] Thus, sub-atomic physics is not a proven exception to premise (1). Second, even on the traditional, indeterministic interpretation, particles do not come into being out of nothing. They arise as spontaneous fluctuations of the energy contained in the sub-atomic vacuum; they do not come from nothing.[13] Third, the same point can be made about theories of the origin of the universe out of a primordial vacuum.[14] Popular magazines touting such theories as getting "something from nothing" simply do not understand that the vacuum is not nothing, but is a sea of fluctuating energy endowed with a rich structure and subject to physical laws. Philosopher of science Robert Deltete accurately sums up the situation: "There is no basis in ordinary quantum theory for the claim that the universe itself is uncaused, much less for the claim that it sprang into being uncaused from literally nothing."[15]

Other atheists have said that premise (1) is true only for things *in* the universe, but it is not true *of* the universe itself. But this objection misconstrues the nature of the premise. Premise (1) does not state merely a physical law like the law of gravity or the laws of thermodynamics, which are valid for things within the universe. Premise (1) is not a physical principle. Rather premise (1) is a metaphysical principle, a principle about the very nature of reality: *Being cannot come from non-being; something cannot come into existence uncaused from nothing.* The principle therefore applies to all of reality. It is thus metaphysically absurd that the universe should pop into being uncaused out of nothing. Even J. L. Mackie, one of the most prominent atheists of our day, admitted that he found such an idea incredible, commenting, "I myself find it hard to accept the notion of self-creation *from nothing*, even given unrestricted chance. And how *can* this be given, if there really is nothing?"[16] Think about it. On the atheistic view, there wasn't even the *potentiality* of the universe's existence prior to the Big Bang, since nothing is prior to the Big Bang. But then how could the universe become actual if there wasn't even the potentiality of its existence? It makes much more sense to say that the potentiality of the universe lay in the power of God to create it.

So what about premise (2) **The universe began to exist**? The typical objection that is raised against the philosophical argument for the universe's beginning is that modern mathematical set theory proves that an actually infinite number of things can exist. For example, there are an actually infinite number of members in the set {0, 1, 2, 3, . . .}. Therefore, there's no problem in an actually infinite number of past events.

But this objection is far too quick. First, not all mathematicians agree that actual infinites exist even in the mathematical realm.[17] They regard series like 0, 1, 2, 3, . . . as merely *potentially* infinite; that is to say, such series approach infinity as a conceptual limit, but they never actually get there. Second, existence in the mathematical realm does not imply existence in the real world. To say that infinite sets exist is merely to postulate a realm of discourse, governed by certain axioms and rules which are simply presupposed, in which one can talk about such collections.[18] Given the axioms and rules, one can discourse consistently about infinite sets. But that's no guarantee that the axioms and rules are *true* or that an actually infinite number of things can exist in the *real* world. Third, in any case the real existence of an actually infinite number of things would violate the rules of infinite set theory. As we saw, trying to subtract infinite quantities leads to self-contradictions; therefore, infinite set theory just prohibits such operations to preserve consistency. But in the real world there's nothing to keep us from breaking this arbitrary rule. If I had an actually infinite number of marbles, I could subtract or divide them as I please—which leads to absurdity.

Sometimes it's said that we can find counter-examples to the claim that an actually infinite number of things cannot exist, so that this claim must be false. For instance, isn't every finite distance capable of being divided into 1/2, 1/4, 1/8, . . . , on to infinity? Doesn't that prove that there are in any finite distance an actually infinite number of parts? The fallacy of this objection is that it once again confuses a potential infinite with an actual infinite. You can continue to divide any distance for as long as you want, but such a series is merely potentially infinite, in that infinity serves as a limit which you endlessly approach but never reach. If you assume that any distance is *already* composed out of an actually infinite number of parts, then you're begging the question. You're assuming what the objector is supposed to prove, namely that there is a clear counter-example to the claim that an actually infinite number of things cannot exist.

As for the scientific confirmation of premise (2), vague references are often made by objectors to alternative theories to the Big Bang theory which do not involve a beginning of the universe. But while such theories are possible, it has been the overwhelming verdict of the scientific community than none of them is more probable than the Big Bang theory. The devil is in the details, and once you get down to specifics, you find that there is no mathematically consistent model which has been so successful in its predictions or as corroborated by the evidence as the traditional Big Bang theory. For example, some theories, like the Oscillating Universe (which expands and re-contracts forever) or the Chaotic Inflationary Universe (which continually spawns new universes), do have a potentially infinite future but turn out to have only a finite past.[19] Vacuum Fluctuation Universe theories (which postulate an eternal vacuum out of which our universe is born) cannot explain why, if the vacuum was eternal, we do not observe an infinitely old universe.[20]

The Quantum Gravity Universe theory propounded by the famous physicist Stephen Hawking, if interpreted realistically, still involves an absolute origin of the universe even if the universe does not begin in a so-called singularity, as it does in the standard Big Bang theory.[21] In sum, according to Hawking, "Almost everyone now believes that the universe, and *time itself*, had a beginning at the Big Bang."[22]

In light of the evidence both the premises of the first argument thus seem more plausible than their denials. Hence, it is plausible that a transcendent Creator of the universe exists.

Sometimes people resist this conclusion because they claim that it is a pseudo-explanation of the origin of the universe. "Just because we can't explain it doesn't mean God did it," they protest. But such a response misconstrues the argument. In the first place, this argument is a *deductive* argument. Therefore, if the premises are true and the logic is valid, the conclusion follows, period. It doesn't matter if it's explanatory or not. The conclusion is entailed by the premises; so you can't object to the conclusion once you have granted the premises. Moreover, in no place does the argument postulate God to plug up a gap in our scientific knowledge. The scientific evidence is used only to confirm the truth of premise (2), which is a religiously neutral statement which can be found in any textbook on astronomy. God's existence is implied only by the conjunction of premise (1) with premise (2). Finally, the hypothesis of God is, in fact, genuinely explanatory, though it is not a scientific, but a personal explanation.[23] It explains some effect in terms of an agent and his intentions. We employ such explanations all the time. For example, if you were to come into the kitchen and find the kettle boiling and asked me, "Why is the kettle boiling?" I might give you an explanation in terms of the kinetic energy communicated to the water by the flame by means of the heat-conducting metal used in the manufacture of the kettle, which causes the molecules of the water in the kettle to vibrate faster and faster until they are thrown off in the form of steam—or I might say, "I put it on to make a cup of tea!" Both are equally legitimate explanations, and in many contexts only a personal explanation will do. In the case of cosmic origins, as Oxford philosopher Richard Swinburne points out, there *cannot* be a scientific explanation of a first state of the universe, since there is nothing before it, and therefore if it lacks a personal explanation, such as our argument provides, then it simply has no explanation at all—which is metaphysically absurd, since on that account the universe just popped into being uncaused out of nothing.

Other atheists have charged that the argument's conclusion is incoherent, since a cause must come before its effect, and there is no moment before the Big Bang. This objection, however, is easy to answer. Many causes and effects are simultaneous. Thus, the moment of God's causing the Big Bang just is the moment of the occurrence of the Big Bang. We can then say that God's existing alone without the universe is either before the Big Bang, not in physical time, but in an undifferentiated metaphysical time or else is strictly timeless but enters into time at the moment of creation. No incoherence has been shown in either of these alternatives.

Sometimes people will say, "But if the universe must have a cause, then what is God's cause?" But this question reveals an inattentiveness to the formulation of the argument. The first premise does not state **Whatever *exists* has a cause**, but rather **Whatever *begins to exist* has a cause**. The difference is important. The insight which lies at the root of premise (1) is that being cannot come from non-being, that something cannot come from nothing. God, since he never began to exist, would not require a cause, for he never came into being. Nor is this special pleading for God, since this is exactly what the atheist has always claimed about the universe: that it is eternal and uncaused. The problem is that the atheist's claim is now rendered untenable in light of the beginning of the universe.

Finally, someone might wonder, "But isn't God supposed to be infinite? And your argument shows that the infinite cannot exist. So how can God exist?" In fact, the argument was that an actually infinite *number of things* cannot exist. And God is not a collection of an actually infinite number of things! As a non-physical being, he doesn't even have parts. When theologians speak of God's infinity, they are thus using the term in a qualitative, not a quantitative sense. They mean that God is absolutely holy, uncreated, self-existent, all-powerful, all-present, and so forth. It's not a mathematical concept. Thus, there's no contradiction.

In sum, we seem to have a good argument for God's existence based upon the origin of the universe.

SECOND REASON

God makes sense of the complex order in the universe.

During the last 30 years or so, scientists have discovered that the existence of intelligent life like ours depends upon a complex and delicate balance of initial conditions given in the Big Bang itself. Scientists once believed that whatever the initial conditions of the universe, eventually intelligent life might evolve. But we now know that our existence is balanced on a knife's edge. It seems vastly more probable that a life-*prohibiting* universe rather than a life-*permitting* universe like ours should exist. The existence of intelligent life depends upon a conspiracy of initial conditions which must be fine-tuned to a degree that is literally incomprehensible and incalculable. For example, Stephen Hawking has estimated that if the rate of the universe's expansion one second after the Big Bang had been smaller by even one part in a hundred thousand million million, the universe would have re-collapsed into a hot fireball.[24] British physicist P.C.W. Davies has calculated that the odds against the initial conditions being suitable for later star formation (without which planets could not exist) is one followed by a thousand billion billion zeroes, at least.[25] He also estimates that a change in the strength of gravity or of the weak force by only one part in 10^{100} would have prevented a life-permitting universe. Another crucial factor is the amount of usable energy in the universe (or the lack thereof, which is *entropy*). Roger Penrose of Oxford University has calculated that the odds of the Big Bang's low entropy condition existing by chance are on the order of one out of $10^{10^{(123)}}$.[26] There are around 50 such quantities and constants present in the Big Bang which must be fine-tuned in this way if the universe is to permit life. And it's not just *each* quantity which must be exquisitely finely-tuned; their *ratios* to one another must be also finely-tuned. So improbability is added to improbability to improbability until our minds are reeling in incomprehensible numbers.

Now there are three possibilities for explaining the presence of this remarkable fine-tuning of the universe: natural law, chance, or design. The first alternative holds that the fine-tuning of the universe is physically necessary. There is some unknown Theory of Everything which would explain the way the universe is. It had to be that way, and there was really no chance or little chance of the universe's not being life-permitting. By contrast, the second alternative states that the fine-tuning is due entirely to chance. It's just an accident that the universe is life-permitting, and we're the lucky beneficiaries. The third alternative rejects both of these accounts in favor of an intelligent Mind behind the cosmos, who designed the universe to permit life. Which of these alternatives is the most plausible?

On the face of it, the first alternative seems extraordinarily implausible. It requires us to believe that a life-*prohibiting* universe is virtually physically *impossible*. But surely it does seem possible. If the matter and anti-matter had been differently proportioned, if the universe had expanded just a little more slowly, if the entropy of the universe were slightly greater, any of these adjustments and more would have prevented a life-permitting universe, yet all seem perfectly possible physically. The person who maintains that the universe must be life-permitting is taking a radical line which requires strong proof. But there is none; this alternative is simply put forward as a bare possibility.

Moreover, there is good reason to reject this alternative. First, there are models of the universe which are different from the existing universe. As John Leslie explains, "The claim that blind necessity is involved— that universes whose laws or constants are slightly different 'aren't real physical possibilities' . . . is eroded by the various physical theories, particularly theories of random symmetry breaking, which *show* how a varied ensemble of universes might be generated."[27] If, as

Leslie suggests, sub-atomic indeterminacy (or uncausedness) is real, then it *must* be possible for the universe to be different, since a number of physical variables depend upon sub-atomic processes which are random in nature. Second, even if the laws of nature were necessary, one would still have to supply initial conditions. As P. C. W. Davies states,

> Even if the laws of physics were unique, it doesn't follow that the physical universe itself is unique. . . . the laws of physics must be augmented by cosmic initial conditions. . . . There is nothing in present ideas about 'laws of initial conditions' remotely to suggest that their consistency with the laws of physics would imply uniqueness. Far from it. . . .
> . . . it seems, then, that the physical universe does not have to be the way it is: it could have been otherwise.[28]

The extraordinarily low entropy condition of the early universe would be a good example of an arbitrary quantity which seems to have just been put in at the creation as an initial condition. Sometimes it is said that we really do not know how much certain constants and quantities could have varied from their actual values. But this admitted uncertainty becomes less important when the number of the variables to be fine-tuned is high. For example, the chances of all 50 known variables being finely-tuned, even if each variable has a 50% chance of being its actual value, is less than 3 out of 10^{17}. Finally, if there is a single, physically possible universe, then the existence of this incredibly complex world-machine might be itself powerful evidence that a Designer exists. Some theorists call the hypothesis that the universe must be life-permitting "the Strong Anthropic Principle," and it is often taken as indicative of God's existence. As physicists Barrow and Tipler write in their *Anthropic Cosmological Principle*, "The Strong Anthropic Principle . . . has strong teleological overtones. This type of notion was extensively discussed in past centuries and was bound up with the question of evidence for a Deity."[29] Thus, the first alternative is not very plausible to begin with and is perhaps indicative of design.

What about the second alternative, that the fine-tuning of the universe is due to chance? The problem with this alternative is that the odds against the fine-tuning's occurring by accident are so incomprehensibly great that they cannot be reasonably faced. Students or laymen who blithely assert that "It could have happened by chance!" simply have no conception of the fantastic precision of the fine-tuning requisite for life. They would never embrace such a hypothesis in any other area of their lives—for example, in order to explain how there came to be overnight a car in one's driveway.

But it's important to understand that it's not just the probability that's at stake here. After all, fantastically improbable events happen every day—your own existence, for example, is the result of an incredibly improbable union of a certain sperm and a certain egg, yet no one would infer that their union was therefore designed. Rather what is at stake in eliminating the hypothesis of chance is what theorists call "specified probability": the demonstration that the event in question is not only improbable but also conforms to an independently discovered pattern.[30] Any sequence of letters hammered out by a chimpanzee seated at a typewriter is equally improbable; but if we find a beautiful sonnet has been typed, then we know that this is not the result of blind chance, since it conforms to the independently given pattern of grammatical English sentences. In the same way, physics and biology tell us independently of any knowledge of the early conditions of the universe what the physical conditions requisite for life are. We then discover how incredibly improbable such conditions are. It is this combination of a specified pattern plus improbability that serves to render the chance hypothesis implausible.

With this in mind, we can immediately see the fallacy of those who say that the existence of any universe is equally improbable and therefore there is nothing here to be explained. It is not the improbability of some universe or other's existing that concerns us; rather it is the specified probability of a life-permitting universe's existing that is at issue. Thus, the proper analogy to the fine-tuning of the universe is not, as defenders of the chance hypothesis often suppose, a lottery in which any individual's winning is fantastically and equally improbable but which some individual has to win. Rather the analogy is a lottery in which a single white ball is mixed into a billion billion billion black balls, and you are asked to reach in and pull out a ball. Any ball you pick will be equally improbable; nevertheless, it is overwhelmingly more probable that whichever ball you pick, it will be black rather than white. Similarly, the existence of any particular universe is equally improbable; but it is incomprehensibly more probable that whichever universe exists, it will be life-prohibiting rather than life-permitting. It is the enormous, specified improbability of the fine-tuning that presents the hurdle for the chance hypothesis.

How can the atheist get over this hurdle? Some thinkers have argued that we really shouldn't be surprised at the finely-tuned conditions of the universe, for if the universe were not fine-tuned, then we wouldn't be here to be surprised about it! Given that we are here, we should expect the universe to be fine-tuned. But such reasoning is logically fallacious. The statement "We shouldn't be surprised that we do not observe conditions of the universe incompatible with our existence" is true. If the conditions of the universe were incompatible with our existence, we couldn't be here to observe them. So it's not surprising that we don't observe such conditions. But from that statement it does not logically follow that "We shouldn't be surprised that we *do* observe conditions of the universe which *are* compatible with our existence." Given the incredible improbability of such finely-tuned conditions, it is surprising that we observe them.

John Leslie provides a charming analogy to illustrate the fallacy of the objector's reasoning. Imagine you're traveling abroad and are arrested on trumped-up drug charges and dragged in front of a firing squad of 100 trained marksmen, all with rifles aimed at your heart, to be executed. You hear the command given: "Ready! Aim! Fire!" and you hear the deafening roar of the guns. And then you observe that you are still alive, that *all* of the 100 trained marksmen missed! Now what would you conclude? "Well, I guess I really shouldn't be surprised that they all missed. After all, if they hadn't all missed, then I wouldn't be here to be surprised about it! Given that I am here, I should *expect* them all to miss." Of course not! You would immediately suspect that they all missed on purpose, that the whole thing was a set-up, engineered for some reason by someone. You wouldn't be surprised that you do not observe that you are dead (since if you were dead, you wouldn't be there to observe it), but you would be quite rightly surprised that you do observe that you are alive (in view of the enormous improbability of all the marksmen's missing). You wouldn't just write off your survival to chance.

Theorists who defend the alternative of chance have therefore been forced to adopt an extraordinary hypothesis: the Many Worlds Hypothesis. According to this hypothesis, our universe is but one member of a greater collection of universes, all of which are real, actually existing universes, not merely possible universes. In order to ensure that somewhere in the World Ensemble there will appear by chance a universe finely-tuned for life, it is further stipulated that there are an infinite number of universes in the collection (so that every possibility will be realized) and that the physical constants and quantities are randomly ordered (so that the worlds are not all alike). Thus, somewhere in this World Ensemble there will appear by chance alone finely-tuned universes like ours. We should not be surprised to observe finely-tuned conditions, since observers like us exist only in those universes which are finely-tuned.

The very fact that detractors of the design hypothesis have to resort to such a remarkable hypothesis underlines the point made earlier that the fine-tuning is not explicable in terms of natural law alone or in terms of sheer chance in the absence of a World Ensemble. The Many Worlds Hypothesis is a sort of backhanded compliment to the design hypothesis in its recognition that the fine-tuning cries out for explanation. But is the Many Worlds Hypothesis as plausible as the design hypothesis?

It seems not. In the first place, it needs to be recognized that the Many Worlds Hypothesis is no more scientific, and no less metaphysical, than the hypothesis of a Cosmic Designer. As the scientist-theologian John Polkinghorne says, "People try to trick out a 'many universe' account in sort of pseudo-scientific terms, but that is pseudo-science. It is a metaphysical guess that there might be many universes with different laws and circumstances."[31] But as a metaphysical hypothesis, the Many Worlds Hypothesis is arguably inferior to the design hypothesis because the design hypothesis is *simpler*. According to a principle known as Ockham's Razor, we should not multiply causes beyond what is necessary to explain the effect. But it is simpler to postulate one Cosmic Designer to explain our universe than to postulate the infinitely bloated collection of universes required by the Many Worlds Hypothesis. Therefore, the design hypothesis is to be preferred. Second, there is no known way for *generating* a World Ensemble. No one has been able to explain how or why such a collection of universes should exist. Moreover, those attempts which have been made require fine-tuning themselves. For example, although some cosmologists appeal to so-called inflationary theories of the universe to generate a World Ensemble, the only consistent inflationary model is Linde's Chaotic Inflationary Theory, and it requires fine-tuning to start the inflation. As Robert Brandenburger of Brown University writes, "Linde's scenario does not address a crucial problem, namely the cosmological constant problem. The field which drives inflation in Linde's scenario is expected to generate an unacceptably large cosmological constant *which must be tuned to zero by hand.* This is a problem which plagues *all* inflationary universe models."[32] Third, there is no *evidence* for the existence of a World Ensemble apart from the fine-tuning itself. But the fine-tuning is equally evidence for a Cosmic Designer. Indeed, the hypothesis of a Cosmic Designer is again the better explanation because we do have independent evidence of the existence of such a Designer in the form of the other arguments for the existence of God. Fourth, the Many Worlds Hypothesis faces a severe challenge from *biological evolutionary theory,* as I'll now explain.[33]

First, a bit of background: During the nineteenth century the German physicist Ludwig Boltzmann proposed a sort of Many Worlds Hypothesis in order to explain why we do not find the universe in a state of "heat death" or thermodynamic equilibrium in which energy is evenly diffused throughout the universe.[34] Boltzmann hypothesized that the universe as a whole *does,* in fact, exist in an equilibrium state, but that over time fluctuations in the energy level occur here and there throughout the universe, so that by chance alone there will be isolated regions where disequilibrium exists. Boltzmann referred to these isolated regions as "worlds." We should not be surprised to see our world in a highly improbable disequilibrium state, since in the ensemble of all worlds there must exist by chance alone certain worlds in disequilibrium, and ours just happens to be one.

The problem with Boltzmann's daring Many Worlds Hypothesis was that if our world were merely a fluctuation in a sea of diffuse energy, then it is overwhelmingly more probable that we would be observing a much tinier region of disequilibrium than we do. In order for us to exist, a smaller fluctuation, even one that produced our world instantaneously by an enormous accident, is inestimably more probable than a progressive decline in entropy to fashion the world we see. In fact, Boltzmann's hypothesis, if adopted, would force us to regard the past as illusory, everything having the mere appearance of age, and the stars and planets as illusory, mere "pictures" as it were, since that sort of world is vastly more probable given a state of overall equilibrium than a world with genuine temporally and spatially distant events. Therefore, Boltzmann's Many Worlds Hypothesis has been universally rejected by the scientific community, and the present disequilibrium is usually taken to be just a result of the initial low entropy condition mysteriously existing at the beginning of the universe.

Now a precisely parallel problem attends the Many Worlds Hypothesis as an explanation of fine-tuning. According to the prevailing theory of biological evolution, intelligent life like ourselves, if it evolves at all, will do so as late in the lifetime of the sun as possible. The less the time span available for the mechanisms of genetic mutation and natural selection to function, the lower the probability of intelligent life's evolving. Given the complexity of the human organism, it is overwhelmingly more probable that human beings will evolve late in the lifetime of the sun rather than early. In fact Barrow and Tipler list ten steps in the evolution of human beings *each of which* is so improbable that before it would occur the sun would have ceased to be a main sequence star and incinerated the Earth![35] Hence, if our universe is but one member of a World Ensemble, then it is overwhelmingly more probable that we should be observing a very old sun rather than a relatively young one of only a few billion years. If we are products of biological evolution, we should find ourselves in a world in which we evolve later in the lifetime of our star. In fact, adopting the Many Worlds Hypothesis to explain away fine-tuning also results in a strange sort of illusionism: it is far more probable that all our astronomical, geological, and biological estimates of age are wrong, that we really do exist very late in the lifetime of the sun and that the sun's and the Earth's appearance of youth is a massive illusion.

The error made by the Many Worlds Hypothesis is what probability theorists call "multiplying one's probabilistic resources without warrant," that is to say, arbitrarily assuming that one has more chances than it appears just to increase the odds of getting some result. If we're allowed to do that, *anything* can be explained away. For example, a cardplayer who gets four aces every time he deals could explain this away by saying that there are an infinite number of universes with poker games going on in them and therefore in some of them someone always by chance gets four aces every time he deals, and—lucky me!—we just happen to be in one of these universes. This sort of arbitrary multiplying of one's probabilistic resources would render rational conduct impossible.

Thus, the Many Worlds Hypothesis collapses and along with it the alternative of chance which it sought to rescue. Both the natural law alternative and the chance alternative are therefore implausible.

We can summarize this second argument as follows:

1. **The fine-tuning of the universe is due to either law, chance, or design.**
2. **It is not due to law or chance.**
3. **Therefore, it is due to design.**

What objections might be raised to the alternative of design? According to this hypothesis there exists a Cosmic Designer who fine-tuned the initial conditions of the universe for intelligent life. Such a hypothesis supplies a personal explanation of the fine-tuning of the universe. Is this explanation implausible?

Detractors of design sometimes object that the Designer Himself remains unexplained. It is said that an intelligent Mind also exhibits complex order, so that if the universe needs an explanation, so does its Designer. If the Designer does not need an explanation, why think that the universe does?

This popular objection is based on a misconception of the nature of explanation. It is widely recognized that in order for an explanation to be the best, one needn't have an explanation of the explanation (indeed, such a requirement would generate an infinite regress, so that everything becomes inexplicable). If the best explanation of a disease is a previously unknown virus, doctors need not be able to explain the virus in order to know it caused the disease. If archaeologists determine that the best explanation of certain artifacts is a lost tribe of ancient people, we needn't be able to explain their origin in order to say justifiably that they produced the artifacts. If astronauts should find traces of intelligent life on some other planet, we need not be able to explain such extra-terrestrials in order to recognize that they are the best explanation. In the same way, the design hypothesis' being the best explanation of the fine-tuning doesn't depend on our being able to explain the Designer.

Moreover, the complexity in a Mind is not really analogous to the complexity of the universe. A mind's *ideas* may be complex, but a mind itself is a remarkably simple thing, being an immaterial entity not composed of parts. Moreover, a mind in order to be a mind must have certain properties like intelligence, consciousness, and volition. These are not contingent properties which it might lack, but are essential to its nature. So it's difficult to see any analogy between the contingently complex universe and a mind. Detractors of design have evidently confused a mind's thoughts (which may be complex) with the mind itself (which is pretty simple). Postulating an uncreated Mind behind the cosmos is thus not at all like postulating an undesigned cosmos.

Sometimes people object to design by pointing to examples of alleged design which we regard as evil or hurtful. For example, it is said that a deadly bacterium or a tapeworm is a complex entity; but how could we ascribe such creatures to a divine Designer?

This objection is simply irrelevant to the design hypothesis, which says nothing about the moral qualities of the Cosmic Designer. A bacterium or even a single flagellum (not to speak of a tapeworm) is so fantastically complex an organism that it cannot be explained in terms of natural law and chance alone.[36] What their existence appears to call into question is not the need of a designer, but the goodness or benevolence of the designer. That is an issue for the next argument we shall consider, the moral argument. To think moral considerations call into question the hypothesis of design would be to say that thumb-screws or a torture rack do not require the existence of intelligent designers!

Thus, the design hypothesis does not share in the implausibility of its competitors and is a familiar sort of explanation which we employ every day. It is there-fore the best explanation of the amazing fine-tuning of our universe.

THIRD REASON

*God makes sense of objective
moral values in the world.*

⚬─⫯─⚬

If God does not exist, then objective moral values
do not exist. When I speak of *objective* moral values,
I mean moral values which are valid and binding
whether anybody believes in them or not. Thus, to
say, for example, that the Holocaust was objectively
wrong is to say that it was wrong even though the
Nazis who carried it out thought that it was right and
that it would still have been wrong even if the Nazis
had won World War II and succeeded in exterminat-
ing or brain-washing everyone who disagreed with
them. Now if God does not exist, then moral values
are not objective in this way.

Many theists and atheists alike concur on this
point. For example, Bertrand Russell observed,

> . . . ethics arises from the pressures of the
> community on the individual. Man . . . does not
> always instinctively feel the desires which are
> useful to his herd. The herd, being anxious that
> the individual should act in its interests, has
> invented various devices for causing the
> individual's interest to be in harmony with that of
> the herd. One of these . . . is morality.[37]

Michael Ruse, a philosopher of science at the
University of Guelph, agrees. He explains,

> Morality is a biological adaptation no less than are
> hands and feet and teeth. Considered as a
> rationally justifiable set of claims about an
> objective something, ethics is illusory. I appreciate
> that when somebody says 'Love thy neighbor as
> thyself,' they think they are referring above and
> beyond themselves. Nevertheless, such reference
> is truly without foundation. Morality is just an aid

to survival and reproduction . . . and any deeper meaning is illusory.[38]

Friedrich Nietzsche, the great atheist of the last century who proclaimed the death of God, understood that the death of God meant the destruction of all meaning and value in life. I think that Friedrich Nietzsche was right.

But we must be very careful here. The question here is *not*: "Must we believe in God in order to live moral lives?" I'm not claiming that we must. Nor is the question: "Can we *recognize* objective moral values without believing in God?" I think that we can. Nor is the question: "Can we formulate an adequate system of ethics without reference to God?" So long as we assume that human beings have objective moral value, the atheist could probably draft a moral code which the theist would largely agree with.

Rather the question is: "If God does not exist, do objective moral values exist?" Like Russell and Ruse, I don't see any reason to think that in the absence of God, the herd morality evolved by *homo sapiens* is objective. After all, if there is no God, then what's so special about human beings? They're just accidental by-products of nature which have evolved relatively recently on an infinitesimal speck of dust lost somewhere in a hostile and mindless universe and which are doomed to perish individually and collectively in a relatively short time. On the atheistic view, some action, say, rape, may not be socially advantageous, and so in the course of human development has become taboo; but that does absolutely nothing to prove that rape is really wrong. On the atheistic view, there's nothing really *wrong* with your raping someone. (In fact, it is quite conceivable that rape could have evolved as an action advantageous for the survival of the species.) Thus, without God there is no absolute right and wrong which imposes itself on our conscience.

But the problem is that objective values *do* exist, and deep down we all know it. There's no more reason to deny the objective reality of moral values than the objective reality of the physical world. As John Healey, the Executive Director of Amnesty International wrote in a fund-raising letter, "I am writing you today because I think you share my profound belief that *there are indeed some moral absolutes.* When it comes to torture, to government-sanctioned murder, to 'disappearances'—there are no lesser evils. These are outrages against all of us."[39] Actions like rape, cruelty, and child abuse aren't just socially unacceptable behavior—they're moral abominations. Some things are really wrong. Similarly love, equality, and self-sacrifice are really good. But if moral values cannot exist without God and moral values do exist, then it follows logically and inescapably that God exists.

We can summarize this argument as follows:

1. **If God does not exist, objective moral values do not exist.**
2. **Objective moral values do exist.**
3. **Therefore, God exists.**

Again, let us consider possible objections which might be raised against this argument.

Some atheist philosophers, unwilling to bite the bullet and affirm that acts like rape or torturing a child are morally neutral actions, have tried to affirm objective moral values in the absence of God, thus in effect denying premise (1). Let's call this alternative Atheistic Moral Realism. Atheistic moral realists affirm that moral values and duties do exist in reality and are not dependent upon evolution or human opinion, but they insist that they are not grounded in God. Indeed, moral values have no further foundation. They just exist.

I must confess that this alternative strikes me as incomprehensible, an example of trying to have your cake and eat it, too. What does it mean to say, for example, that the moral value *Justice* just exists? I don't know what this means. I understand what it is for a person to be just; but I draw a complete blank when it is said that, in the absence of any persons, *Justice* itself exists. Moral values seem to exist as properties of persons, not as abstractions—or at any rate, I don't know what it is for a moral value to exist as an abstraction. Atheistic moral realists seem to lack any adequate foundation in reality for moral values but just leave them floating in an unintelligible way.

Second, the nature of moral duty or obligation seems incompatible with Atheistic Moral Realism. Let's suppose for the sake of argument that moral values do exist independently of God. Suppose that values like *Mercy, Justice, Love, Forbearance*, and the like just exist. How does that result in any moral obligations for me? Why would I have a moral duty, say, to be merciful? Who or what lays such an obligation on me? As the ethicist Richard Taylor points out, "A duty is something that is owed . . . . But something can be owed only to some person or persons. There can be no such thing as duty in isolation . . . ."[40] God makes sense of moral obligation because his commands constitute for us our moral duties. Taylor writes, "Our moral obligations can . . . be understood as those that are imposed by God . . . . But what if this higher-than-human lawgiver is no longer taken into account? Does the concept of a moral obligation . . . still make sense? . . . the concept of moral obligation [is] unintelligible apart from the idea of God. The words remain but their meaning is gone."[41] According to Taylor, we literally have no moral obligations; there is no right or wrong. The Atheistic Moral Realist rightly finds this abhorrent, but, as Taylor clearly sees, on an atheistic view there simply is no ground for duty, even if moral values somehow exist.

Thirdly, it is fantastically improbable that just that sort of creatures would emerge from the blind evolutionary process who correspond to the abstractly existing realm of moral values. This seems to be an utterly incredible coincidence when you think about it. It is almost as though the moral realm *knew* that we were coming. It is far more plausible to regard both the natural realm and the moral realm as under the hegemony or authority of a divine Designer and Lawgiver than to think that these two entirely independent orders of reality just happened to mesh.

Thus it seems to me that Atheistic Moral Realism is not a plausible view, but is basically a halfway house for philosophers who don't have the stomach for the moral nihilism or meaninglessness which their own atheism implies.

What, then, about premise (2) **Objective moral values do exist**? Some people, as we have seen, deny that objective moral values exist. I agree with them that IF there is no God, then moral values are just the products of socio-biological evolution or expressions of personal taste. But I see no reason to think that that is in fact all that moral values are. Those who think so seem to commit the genetic fallacy, which is trying to invalidate something by showing how it *originated*. For example, a socialist who tried to refute your belief in democratic government by saying, "The only reason you believe in democracy is that you were raised in a democratic society!" would be guilty of the genetic fallacy. For even if it were true that your belief is totally the result of cultural conditioning, that does absolutely nothing to show that your belief is false (think of people who have been culturally conditioned to believe that the Earth is round!). The truth of an idea is not dependent upon how that idea originated. It's the same with moral values. If moral values are *discovered* rather than *invented*, then our gradual and fallible apprehension of the moral realm no more undermines the objective reality of that realm than our gradual, fallible apprehension of the physical world undermines the objective reality of the physical realm. We know objective moral values exist because we clearly apprehend some of them. The best way to show this is simply to describe moral situations in which we clearly see right and wrong: torturing a child, incest, rape, ethnic cleansing, racism, witch-burning, the Inquisition, and so forth. If someone really fails to see the objective moral truth about such matters, then he is simply morally handicapped, like a color-blind person who cannot tell the difference between red and green, and there's no reason to think that his impairment should make us call into question what we see clearly.

From the truth of the two premises the conclusion follows logically that (3) **Therefore, God exists**. Now many atheists have objected to basing moral values in God. Sometimes it is said that when we affirm, "God is good," we must have some independent meaning of the word "good." For if "good" is defined just in terms of the way God is, then to say "God is good" is just to say "God is the way God is," which is trivial.

This objection, however, confuses the order of *knowing* with the order of *being*. In the order of knowing, it is true that we do not derive our concept of "Good" from God. We learn what goodness means through experience in the world and with other people. But that doesn't address the question of where goodness itself comes from. In the order of knowing, the concept of goodness may come before the concept of God; but in the order of being goodness is rooted in God.

Frequently an argument from Plato known as the Euthyphro Argument is brought against basing values in God. The argument presents a dilemma: either something is good because God commands it or else God commands something because it is good. If you say something is good because God commands it, this makes right and wrong arbitrary; God could have commanded that acts of hatred, brutality, cruelty, and so on be good, and then we would be morally obligated to do such things, which seems crazy. On the other hand, if God commands something because it is good, then the Good is independent of God after all. Thus, morality can't be based on God's commands.

Plato himself saw the solution to this objection: you split the horns of the dilemma by formulating a third alternative, namely, God is the Good. The Good is the moral nature of God himself. That is to say, God *is* necessarily holy, loving, kind, just, and so on, and these attributes of God comprise the Good. God's moral character expresses itself toward us in the form of certain commandments, which become for us our moral duties. Hence, God's commandments are not arbitrary, but necessarily flow from his own nature. They are necessary expressions of the way God is.

The atheist might press, "But why think that God's nature constitutes the Good?" Now in one sense, the answer to that question is that there just isn't anything else available. There has to be some explanatory ultimate, some stopping point, and we've seen that without God there are no objective moral values. Therefore, if there are objective moral values, they cannot be based in anything but God! In addition, however, God's nature is an appropriate stopping point for the standard of goodness. For by definition, God is a being who is *worthy of worship*. When you think about what it means to worship someone, then it is evident that only a being which is the embodiment of all moral goodness is worthy to be worshiped.

Thus, God makes sense of ethics in a way that atheism really cannot. So in addition to the metaphysical and scientific arguments for God, we have a powerful moral argument for God.

This moral argument also helps to solve the problem raised by the design argument concerning the moral character of the Designer of the universe. We now see that moral evil in the world does not disprove God's goodness; on the contrary it actually *proves* it. For we may argue:

1. **If God does not exist, objective moral values do not exist.**
2. **Evil exists.**
3. **Therefore, objective moral values exist** (some things are truly evil).
4. **Therefore, God exists.**

Thus, evil paradoxically goes to prove God's existence, since without God things would not be good or evil. Notice that this argument thus shows the compatibility of God and evil without giving a clue as to *why* God permits evil. That is a wholly separate question which has been addressed elsewhere.[42] But even in the absence of any answer to the why question, the present argument proves that evil does not call into question, but actually requires, God's existence.

FOURTH REASON

*God makes sense of the life, death,
and resurrection of Jesus*

—•—

The historical person Jesus of Nazareth was a remarkable individual. New Testament critics have reached something of a consensus that the historical Jesus came on the scene with an unprecedented sense of divine authority, the authority to stand and speak in God's place. That's why the Jewish leadership instigated his crucifixion for the charge of blasphemy—in effect, for slandering God. He claimed that in himself the Kingdom of God had come, and as visible demonstrations of this fact he carried out a ministry of miracle-working and exorcisms. But the supreme confirmation of his claim was his resurrection from the dead. If Jesus did rise from the dead, then it would seem that we have a divine miracle on our hands and, thus, evidence for the existence of God.

Now in discussing this issue, I'm not going to treat the New Testament as an inspired and therefore inerrant book, but simply as a collection of ordinary, Greek documents coming down to us out of the first century. I'm not interested, therefore, in defending the infallibility of the gospels. Rather I'm interested in determining, first, what facts concerning the fate of Jesus of Nazareth can be credibly established on the basis of the evidence and, second, what is the best explanation of those facts.

So let's look at that first question. There are at least four facts about the fate of the historical Jesus which are widely accepted by New Testament historians today. It's worth emphasizing that I'm not talking just about conservative scholars, but about the broad mainstream of New Testament scholarship.

Fact #1: After his crucifixion Jesus was buried by Joseph of Arimathea in a tomb. This fact is highly significant because it means that the location of Jesus' tomb was known to Jew and Christian alike in

41

Jerusalem. New Testament researchers have established the fact of Jesus' honorable burial on the basis of evidence such as the following:

1. Jesus' burial is attested in the very old information which was handed on by Paul in his first letter to the church in Corinth, Greece. Near the end of his letter Paul writes,

For I delivered to you as of first importance what I also received:

> that Christ died for our sins in accordance
>   with the Scriptures,
> and that he was buried,
> and that he was raised on the third day in
>   accordance with the Scriptures,
> and that he appeared to Cephas, then
>   to the Twelve (I Cor. 15:3-5).

This saying, handed on by Paul, is filled with Semitic expressions not of Paul's own style. It has been dated to within five years after Jesus' crucifixion. Notice that the second line refers to Jesus' burial. Comparison of this four-line formula to the gospel narratives on the one hand and to the apostles' sermons in the book of the Acts of the Apostles on the other reveals that the second line is a summary in outline form of the story of Jesus' burial by Joseph in the tomb.

2. The burial story is part of very old source material used by Mark in writing his gospel. Mark is generally acknowledged to be the earliest of the gospels, and obviously his source material goes back even closer to the events of Jesus' life. We thus have very early, independent attestation of the burial in both Mark and Paul.

3. As a member of the Jewish high court that condemned Jesus, Joseph of Arimathea is unlikely to be a Christian invention. There was an understandable hostility in the early Christian movement toward the Jewish leaders, who, in Christian eyes, had engineered a judicial murder of Jesus. Thus, according to

the late New Testament scholar Raymond Brown, Jesus' honorable burial by Joseph is "very probable," since a Christian fictional creation of a Jewish Sanhedrist who does what is right by Jesus "is almost inexplicable."[43]

4. The burial story lacks any signs of legendary development. Even Rudolph Bultmann, one of the most skeptical New Testament scholars of this century, declared, "This is an historical account which creates no impression of being a legend, apart from the women witnesses."[44] The eminent scholar of the book of Mark, Vincent Taylor, says that even Bultmann's assessment is "a notable understatement . . . . The narrative belongs to the best tradition."[45]

5. No other competing burial story exists. If the story of Jesus' burial were a legendary fiction which arose much later than the original event, then it's strange that we have no traces at all of the real account or even competing legendary stories. The unanimity of the burial traditions speaks in favor of the reliability of the gospel account.

For these and other reasons, the majority of New Testament critics concur that Jesus was buried by Joseph of Arimathea in a tomb. According to the late John A. T. Robinson of Cambridge University, the burial of Jesus in the tomb is "one of the earliest and best-attested facts about Jesus."[46]

Fact #2: On the Sunday after the crucifixion, Jesus' tomb was found empty by a group of his women followers. Among the reasons which have led most scholars to this conclusion are the following:

1. The old information transmitted by Paul implies the empty tomb. It does so in two ways. First, the expression "he was raised" following the expression "he was buried" implies an empty grave. A first-century Jew could not have thought otherwise. The fact that reference is being made here to Jesus' empty tomb is evident by comparing again this four-point outline to the gospel narratives and to Acts: the third line is a summary of the empty tomb narrative.

Second, the expression "on the third day" probably is a reference to the day of the women's discovery of the empty tomb. Very briefly summarized, the question here is why the resurrection came to be dated "on the third day." Why not on the tenth day? Or the seventh day? The most probable answer is that it was on the third day after the crucifixion, according to Jewish reckoning, that the women discovered the tomb empty; and so naturally the resurrection came to be dated on that day. Thus, in Paul's information we have two extremely early indications of the fact of the empty tomb.

2.   The empty tomb story is also part of Mark's very old source material. Mark's source did not end with Jesus' burial, but with the empty tomb narrative, which is tied to the burial account verbally and grammatically. Thus, we have very early, independent attestation of the fact of the empty tomb.

3.   The story is simple and lacks signs of legendary embellishment. In Mark's account the women come to the tomb early Sunday morning and find the stone rolled away and the tomb empty. They see an angelic figure who proclaims to them that Jesus is risen and will appear to them in Galilee. They then flee from the tomb in terror and silence. Now to appreciate the simplicity of this account, one has only to compare it to the accounts of the forged apocryphal gospels of the second century and beyond. For example, in the so-called Gospel of Peter, the tomb is encompassed by a Roman guard, all the Jewish chief priests and Pharisees, as well as a huge crowd from the surrounding countryside. Suddenly, during the night a voice rings out from heaven, and the stone over the tomb rolls back by itself from the door. Then two angels descend out of heaven and enter the tomb. Then Jesus himself comes out of the tomb, upheld by the two angels. The heads of the two angels reach up to the clouds, but the head of Jesus overpasses the clouds. Then a cross comes out of the tomb, and a voice from heaven asks, "Hast thou preached to them that sleep?" And the cross answers, "Yea." This is how

real legends look: They are colored by all sorts of apologetical and theological motifs which are conspicuously missing from the account in Mark. At the very most we would only want to delete from Mark's account the angelic figure as an embellishment, and what remains is stark in its simplicity.

4. The tomb was probably discovered empty by women. In Jewish society the testimony of women was regarded as so unreliable that they were not even permitted to serve as witnesses in a Jewish court of law. Now in light of this fact, how remarkable that it is *women* who are the discoverers of Jesus' empty tomb! Any later legendary account would certainly have made male disciples like Peter and John discover the empty tomb. The fact that it is women, rather than men, who are the chief witnesses to the fact of the empty tomb is best explained by the fact that they *were* the discoverers of the empty tomb, and the gospel writers faithfully record what, for them, was an awkward and embarrassing fact.

5. The earliest known Jewish response to the proclamation of Jesus' resurrection presupposes the empty tomb. In the gospel of Matthew, chapter 28, we find the earliest Jewish response to the disciples' proclamation of the resurrection. What were Jews saying in reaction to the disciples' declaration that "He is risen from the dead!"? That these men were full of new wine? That Jesus' body still lay in the tomb in the hillside? No. They said, "The disciples came and stole away his body" (Matt. 28:13-15). Think about that for a second. "The disciples came and stole away his body." The earliest Jewish response to the proclamation of the resurrection was itself an attempt to explain why the body was missing! Thus we have evidence for the empty tomb from the very opponents of the early Christian movement.

I could go on, but I think enough has been said to indicate why, in the words of Jacob Kremer, an Austrian specialist on the resurrection, "By far most exegetes hold firmly to the reliability of the biblical statements concerning the empty tomb."[47]

Fact #3: On multiple occasions and under various circumstances different individuals and groups of people experienced appearances of Jesus alive from the dead. This is a fact which is virtually universally acknowledged among New Testament scholars, for the following reasons:

1. The list of eyewitnesses to Jesus' resurrection appearances which is quoted by Paul guarantees that such appearances occurred. The old formula quoted by Paul goes on to say:

> . . . then he appeared to Cephas, then to the Twelve. Then he appeared to more than 500 brethren at one time, most of whom are still alive, though some have died. Then he appeared to James, then to all the apostles. Last of all, as to one untimely born, he appeared also to me (I Cor. 15:5-8).

Given the early date of this information as well as Paul's personal acquaintance with the people involved, such appearances cannot be dismissed as legendary, but must refer to actual events.

2. The appearance narratives in the gospels provide multiple, independent attestation of the appearances. For example, the appearance to Peter is attested by Luke and Paul; the appearance to the Twelve is attested by Luke, John, and Paul; the appearance to the women is attested by Matthew and John; and appearances in Galilee are attested by Mark, Matthew, and John. The appearance narratives span such a breadth of independent sources that even if it is impossible to prove the historicity of a particular appearance story, nevertheless it cannot be reasonably denied that the earliest disciples did have such experiences.

Even the skeptical German New Testament critic Gerd Lüdemann therefore concludes, "It may be taken as historically certain that Peter and the disciples had experiences after Jesus' death in which Jesus appeared to them as the risen Christ."[48]

Fact #4: The original disciples suddenly and sincerely came to believe that Jesus was risen from the dead despite their having every predisposition to the contrary. Think of the situation the disciples faced following Jesus' crucifixion:

1. Their leader was dead. And Jewish Messianic expectations included no idea of a Messiah who, instead of triumphing over Israel's enemies, would be shamefully executed by them as a criminal.

2. According to Old Testament law, Jesus' execution exposed him as a heretic, a man literally accursed by God.

3. Jewish beliefs about the afterlife precluded anyone's rising from the dead to glory and immortality before the general resurrection of the dead at the end of the world.

Nevertheless, the original disciples suddenly came to believe so strongly that God had raised Jesus from the dead that they were willing to die for the truth of that belief. Luke Johnson, a New Testament scholar at Emory University, states, "Some sort of powerful, transformative experience is required to generate the sort of movement earliest Christianity was."[49] N. T. Wright, an eminent British scholar, concludes, "That is why, as an historian, I cannot explain the rise of early Christianity unless Jesus rose again, leaving an empty tomb behind him."[50]

In summary, then, there are four facts concerning the fate of Jesus of Nazareth which are agreed upon by the majority of scholars who have written on this subject: Jesus' burial by Joseph of Arimathea, the discovery of his empty tomb, his post-mortem appearances, and the origin of the disciples' belief in his resurrection.

But that leads to our second concern: what is the best explanation of these facts? I think that the best explanation in this case is the one that was given by the eyewitnesses: God raised Jesus from the dead. In his book *Justifying Historical Descriptions*, historian C. B. McCullagh lists six tests which historians use in determining what is the best explanation for a given body of historical facts.[51] The hypothesis "God raised Jesus from the dead" passes all these tests.

1. It has great *explanatory scope*: it explains why the tomb was found empty, why the disciples saw post-mortem appearances of Jesus, and why the Christian faith came into being.

2. It has great *explanatory power*: it explains why the body of Jesus was gone, why people repeatedly saw Jesus alive despite his earlier public execution, and so forth.

3. It is *plausible*: given the historical context of Jesus' own unparalleled life and claims, the resurrection makes sense as the divine confirmation of those radical claims.

4. It is *not ad hoc or contrived*: it requires only one additional hypothesis: that God exists.

5. It is *in accord with accepted beliefs*: the hypothesis "God raised Jesus from the dead" does not in any way conflict with the accepted belief that people don't rise *naturally* from the dead. The Christian accepts that belief as wholeheartedly as he accepts the hypothesis that God raised Jesus from the dead.

6. It *far outstrips any of its rival theories* in meeting conditions (1)-(5). Down through history various alternative explanations of the facts have been offered, for example, the conspiracy theory, the apparent death theory, the hallucination theory, and so forth. Such hypotheses have been almost universally rejected by contemporary scholarship. No naturalistic hypothesis has, in fact, attracted a great number of scholars.

Thus, the best explanation of the established facts seems to be that God raised Jesus from the dead. Now, admittedly, such a conclusion would probably be regarded by most scholars as lying beyond the reach of a strict historian. Not that they have any better explanation to offer: all the old theories like "the disciples stole the body" or "Jesus wasn't really dead" have been universally rejected by contemporary scholarship. The fact is that there just is no plausible naturalistic explanation of these facts. Those who are reluctant to infer the resurrection of Jesus are simply self-confessedly left with *no* explanation.

I can understand the historian's reservations on this matter. As a historian one may simply choose to remain agnostic. But surely insofar as we are not merely historians, but human beings searching for the meaning of our existence—travelers, rather than merely balconeers—we cannot be debarred from drawing such a conclusion. Given the admitted failure of all naturalistic explanations, the rational person can hardly be blamed if he concludes that on that first Easter morning a divine miracle occurred.

Moreover, we may push the question a notch further and ask why most historians would have reservations about the resurrection hypothesis. The answer is very simple: the resurrection is a miracle, and in the words of Gerd Lüdemann, "Historical criticism . . . does not reckon with an intervention of God in history."[52] Thus, the resurrection *cannot* be historically established; it is excluded before you even sit down at the table to look at the evidence. Now what justification does Lüdemann give for this crucial presupposition of the impossibility of miracles? All he offers is a couple of one-sentence allusions to Hume and Kant. He says, "Hume . . . demonstrated that a miracle is defined in such a way that 'no testimony is sufficient to establish it.' "[53] The miraculous conception of the resurrection, he says, presupposes "a philosophical realism that has been untenable since Kant."[54] Now Professor Lüdemann is not a philosopher; he's a New Testament theologian. And his procedure here of merely dropping names of famous philosophers is sadly all too typical of theologians. Thomas Morris, a philosopher, comments in his book *Philosophy and the Christian Faith*,

> What is particularly interesting about the references theologians make to Kant or Hume is that most often we find the philosopher merely mentioned . . . , but we rarely, if ever, see an account of precisely which arguments of his are supposed to have accomplished the alleged

demolition . . . . In fact, I must confess to never having seen in the writings of any contemporary theologian the exposition of a single argument from either Hume or Kant, or any other historical figure for that matter, which comes anywhere near to demolishing . . . historical Christian doctrine, or . . . theological realism . . . . [55]

Hume's argument against miracles was already refuted in the 18th century by Paley, Less, and Campbell, and most contemporary philosophers also reject it as fallacious, including such prominent philosophers of science as Richard Swinburne and John Earman and analytic philosophers such as George Mavrodes and William Alston.[56] Even the atheist philosopher Antony Flew, himself a Hume scholar, admits that Hume's argument is defective as it stands.[57] As for philosophical realism, this is actually the *dominant* view among philosophers today. Thus, Lüdemann's rejection of the historicity of miracles on the basis of Hume and Kant represents a groundless presupposition. Reject that presupposition, and it's pretty hard to deny that the resurrection of Jesus is the best explanation of the facts.

Thus, it seems to me that we have a good inductive argument for the existence of God based on the evidence for the resurrection of Jesus. It may be summarized as follows:

1. There are four established facts concerning the fate of Jesus of Nazareth: his honorable burial by Joseph of Arimathea, the discovery of his empty tomb, his post-mortem appearances, and the origin of his disciples' belief in his resurrection.
2. The hypothesis "God raised Jesus from the dead" is the best explanation of these facts.
3. The hypothesis "God raised Jesus from the dead" entails that God exists.
4. Therefore God exists.

FIFTH REASON

God can be immediately known and experienced.

This isn't really an argument for God's existence; rather it's the claim that we can know that God exists wholly apart from arguments simply by immediately experiencing Him. This was the way people described in the Bible knew God, as Professor John Hick explains:

> God was known to them as a dynamic will interacting with their own wills, a sheer given reality, as inescapably to be reckoned with as destructive storm and life-giving sunshine . . . . They did not think of God as an inferred entity but as an experienced reality. . . . To them God was not a proposition completing a syllogism, or an idea adopted by the mind, but the experiential reality which gave significance to their lives.[58]

For these people God was not inferred to be the best explanation of their religious experience and so they believed in Him; rather in their religious experience they came to know God *directly*.

Philosophers call beliefs like this "properly basic beliefs." They aren't based on some other beliefs; rather they are part of the foundation of a person's system of beliefs. Other properly basic beliefs would be the belief in the reality of the past, the existence of the external world, and the presence of other minds like your own. When you think about it, none of these beliefs can be proved. How could you prove that the world was not created five minutes ago with built-in appearances of age like food in our stomachs from the breakfasts we never really ate and memory traces in our brains of events we never really experienced? How could you prove that you are not a brain in a vat of chemicals being stimulated with electrodes by some mad scientist to believe that you are here reading this booklet? How could you prove that other people are not really automata who exhibit all the external behavior of persons with minds, when in reality they are soulless, robot-like entities?

Although these sorts of beliefs are basic for us, that doesn't mean that they're arbitrary. Rather they are grounded in the sense that they're formed in the context of certain experiences. In the experiential context of seeing and feeling and hearing things, I naturally form the belief that there are certain physical objects which I am sensing. Thus, my basic beliefs are not arbitrary, but appropriately grounded in experience. There may be no way to prove such beliefs, and yet it is perfectly rational to hold them. You would have to be crazy to think that the world was created five minutes ago or to believe that you are a brain in a vat! Such beliefs are thus not merely basic, but *properly* basic.

In the same way, belief in God is for those who seek him a properly basic belief grounded in our experience of God, as we discern him in nature, conscience, and other means. Now someone might object that an atheist or an adherent to some non-personal religious faith like Taoism could also claim to know their beliefs in a properly basic way. Certainly, they could *claim* such a thing; but what does that prove? Imagine that you were locked in a room with four color-blind people, all of whom claimed that there is no difference between red and green. Suppose you tried to convince them by showing them colored pictures of red and green objects and asking, "Can't you *see* the difference?" Of course, they would see no difference at all and would dismiss your claim to see different colors as delusory. In terms of *showing* who's right, there would be a complete stand-off. But would their denial of the difference between red and green or your inability to show them that you are right do anything logically either to render your belief false or to invalidate your experience? Obviously not! In the same way the person who has actually come to know God as a living reality in his life can know with assurance that his experience is no delusion, regardless of what the atheist or Taoist tells him. In a recent discussion,[59] philosopher William Alston points out that in such a situation neither party knows how to demonstrate to the other that he alone has a veridical (true), rather than delusory, experience. But this stand-off does not undermine the rationality of belief in God, for *even if the believer's process of forming his belief were as reliable as can be*, he'd still have no way of giving a non-circular proof of this fact. Thus, the believer's inability to provide such a proof does not nullify the rationality of his belief. Still it remains the case that in such a situation although the believer may *know* that his belief is true, both parties are at a complete loss to *show* the truth of their respective beliefs to the other party. How is one to break this deadlock? Alston answers that the believer should do whatever is feasible to find common ground, like logic and empirical facts, by means of which he can show in a non-circular way whose view is correct. That is exactly the procedure which I have sought to follow in this booklet. I know that God exists in a properly basic way, and I've tried to show that God exists by appeal to the common facts of science, ethics, history, and philosophy.

Now if, through experiencing God, we can know in a properly basic way that God exists, then there's a real danger that proofs for God could actually distract one's attention from God himself. If you're sincerely seeking God, God will make His existence evident to you. The Bible promises, "Draw near to God and he will draw near to you"(James 4:8). We mustn't so concentrate on the proofs for God that we fail to hear the inner voice of God to our own heart. For those who listen, God becomes an immediate reality in their lives.

CONCLUSION

In summary, we've seen five good reasons to think that God exists:

1. God makes sense of the origin of the universe.
2. God makes sense of the fine-tuning of the universe for intelligent life.
3. God makes sense of objective moral values in the world.
4. God makes sense of the life, death, and resurrection of Jesus.
5. God can be immediately known and experienced.

These are only a part of the evidence for God's existence. Alvin Plantinga, one of America's leading philosophers, has laid out two dozen or so arguments for God's existence.[60] Together these constitute a powerful cumulative case for the existence of God.

Now if we are travelers and not merely balconeers, the conclusion that God exists is but the first step of our journey, albeit a crucial one. The Bible says, "He who would come to God must believe that he exists and that he is a rewarder of those who seek him" (Hebrews 11:6). If we have come to believe that he exists, we must now seek him, in the confidence that if we do so with our whole heart, he will reward us with the personal knowledge of himself.

ENDNOTES

[1]See James Collins, *God in Modern Philosophy* (Chicago: Henry Regnery, 1959).

[2]Private communication.

[3]Bertrand Russell, *Selected Papers of Bertrand Russell* (New York: Random House, 1927), p. 3.

[4]J. I. Packer, *Knowing God* (London: Hodder & Stoughton, 1973), pp. 5-6.

[5]Thomas Nagel, *The Last Word* (Oxford: Oxford University Press, 1997), p. 130.

[6]David Hilbert, "On the Infinite," in *Philosophy of Mathematics*, ed. with an Introduction by Paul Benacerraf and Hillary Putnam (Englewood Cliffs, N.J.: Prentice-Hall, 1964), pp. 139, 141.

[7]Fred Hoyle, *Astronomy and Cosmology* (San Francisco: W.H. Freeman, 1975), p. 658.

[8]Anthony Kenny, *The Five Ways: St. Thomas Aquinas' Proofs of God's Existence* (New York: Schocken Books, 1969), p. 66.

[9]David Hume to John Stewart, February, 1754, in *The Letters of David Hume*, 2 vols., ed. J. Y. T. Greig (Oxford: Clarendon Press, 1932), I: 187.

[10]Kai Nielsen, *Reason and Practice* (New York: Harper & Row, 1971), p. 48.

[11]Arthur Eddington, *The Expanding Universe* (New York: Macmillan, 1933), p. 124.

[12]See James T. Cushing, Arthur Fine, and Sheldon Goldstein, *Bohmian Mechanics and Quantum Theory: An Appraisal*, Boston Studies in the Philosophy of Science 184 (Dordrecht: Kluwer Academic Publishers, 1996).

[13]See John Barrow and Frank Tipler, *The Anthropic Cosmological Principle* (Oxford: Clarendon Press, 1986), p. 441.

[14]See Bernulf Kanitscheider, "Does Physical Cosmology Transcend the Limits of Naturalistic Reasoning?" in *Studies on Mario Bunge's "Treatise,"* ed. P. Weingartner and G. J. W. Dorn (Amsterdam: Rodopi, 1990), pp. 346-347.

[15]Robert Deltete, critical notice of *Theism, Atheism, and Big Bang Cosmology, Zygon* 30 (1995): 656. (N.B. the review was attributed to J. Leslie due to an editorial mistake at *Zygon.*)

[16]J. L. Mackie, *Times Literary Supplement*, (5 February 1982), p. 126.

[17]See, for example, Abraham Robinson, "Metamathematical Problems," *Journal of Symbolic Logic* 38 (1973): 500-516.

[18]See Alexander Abian, *The Theory of Sets and Transfinite Arithmetic* (Philadelphia: W. B. Saunders, 1965), p. 68; B. Rotman and G. T. Kneebone, *The Theory of Sets and Transfinite Numbers* (London: Oldbourne, 1966), p. 61.

[19]See I. D. Novikov and Y. B. Zeldovich, "Physical Processes near Cosmological Singularities," *Annual Review of Astronomy and Astrophysics* 11 (1973): 401-402; A. Borde and A. Vilenkin, "Eternal Inflation and the Initial Singularity," *Physical Review Letters* 72 (1994): 3305, 3307.

[20]Christopher Isham, "Creation of the Universe as A Quantum Process," in *Physics, Philosophy and Theology: A Common quest for Understanding*, ed. R. J. Russell, W. R. Stoeger, and G. V. Coyne (Vatican City: Vatican Observatory, 1988), pp. 385-387.

[21]See John D. Barrow, *Theories of Everything* (Oxford: Clarendon Press, 1991), pp. 67-68.

[22]Stephen Hawking and Roger Penrose, *The Nature of Space and Time*, The Isaac Newton Institute Series of Lectures (Princeton, N. J.: Princeton University Press, 1996), p. 20.

[23]On this distinction, see the discussion by Richard Swinburne, *The Existence of God*, rev. ed. (Oxford: Clarendon Press, 1991), pp. 32-48.

[24]Stephen W. Hawking, *A Brief History of Time* (New York: Bantam Books, 1988), p. 123.

[25]P. C. W. Davies, *Other Worlds* (London: Dent, 1980), pp. 160-161, 168-169.

[26]P. C. W. Davies, "The Anthropic Principle," in *Particle and Nuclear Physics* 10 (1983): 28.

[27]John Leslie, *Universes* (London: Routledge, 1989), p. 202.

[28]Paul Davies, *The Mind of God* (New York: Simon & Schuster, 1992), p. 169.

[29]Barrow and Tipler, *Anthropic Cosmological Principle*, p. 15.

[30]See William A. Dembski, *The Design Inference: Eliminating Chance through Small Probabilities*, Cambridge Studies in Probability, Induction, and Decision Theory (Cambridge: Cambridge University Press, 1998), pp. 167-174.

[31]Polkinghorne, *Serious Talk*, p. 6

[32]Robert Brandenburger, personal communication.

[33]I owe this insight to the philosopher of science Robin Collins.

[34]Ludwig Boltzmann, *Lectures on Gas Theory*, trans. Stephen G. Brush (Berkeley: University of California Press, 1964), pp. 446-448.

[35]Barrow and Tipler, *Anthropic Cosmological Principle*, pp. 561-565.

[36]See Michael Behe, *Darwin's Black Box* (New York: Free Press, 1996), pp. 51-73.

[37]Bertrand Russell, *Human Society in Ethics and Politics* (New York: Simon and Schuster, 1955), p. 124.

[38]Michael Ruse, "Evolutionary Theory and Christian Ethics," in *The Darwinian Paradigm* (London: Routledge, 1989), pp. 262-269.

[39]John Healey, fund-raising letter, 1991.

[40]Richard Taylor, *Ethics, Faith, and Reason* (Englewood Cliffs, N. J.: Prentice-Hall, 1985), p. 83.

[41]Ibid., pp. 83-84.

[42]See Douglas Geivett, *Can a Good God Allow Evil?*, in this same booklet series.

[43]Raymond E. Brown, *The Death of the Messiah*, 2 vols. (Garden City, N.Y.: Doubleday, 1994), 2: 1240-1241.

[44]Rudolf Bultmann, *The History of the Synoptic Tradition*, 2d ed., trans. John Marsh (Oxford: Basil Blackwell, 19), p. 274.

[45]Vincent Taylor, *The Gospel according to St. Mark*, 2nd ed. (London: Macmillan, 1966), p. 599.

[46]John A. T. Robinson, *The Human Face of God* (Philadelphia: Westminster, 1973), p. 131.

[47]Jacob Kremer, *Die Osterevangelien—Geschichten um Geschichte* (Stuttgart: Katholisches Bibelwerk, 1977), pp. 49-50.

[48]Gerd Lüdemann, *What Really Happened to Jesus?*, trans. John Bowden (Louisville, Kent.: Westminster John Knox Press, 1995), p. 8.

[49]Luke Timothy Johnson, *The Real Jesus* (San Francisco: Harper San Francisco, 1996), p. 136.

[50]N. T. Wright, "The New Unimproved Jesus" *Christianity Today* (September 13, 1993), p. 26.

[51]C. Behan McCullagh, *Justifying Historical Descriptions* (Cambridge: Cambridge University Press, 1984), p. 19.

[52]Gerd Lüdemann, "Die Auferstehung Jesu," in *Fand die Auferstehung wirklich statt?*, ed. Alexander Bommarius (Düsseldorf: Parega Verlag, 1995), p. 16.

[53]Gerd Lüdemann, *The Resurrection of Jesus*, trans. John Bowden (Minneapolis: Fortress Press, 1994), p. 12.

[54]Ibid., p. 249.

[55]Thomas V. Morris, *Philosophy and the Christian Faith*, University of Notre Dame Studies in the Philosophy of Religion 5 (Notre Dame, Ind.: University of Notre Dame Press, 1988), pp. 3-4.

[56]See George Campbell, *Dissertation on Miracles* (1762). Reprint: London: T. Tegg & Son, 1834;

Gottfried Less, *Wahrheit der christlichen Religion* (Göttingen: G. L. Förster, 1776); William Paley, *A View of the Evidences of Christianity*, 2 vols., 5th ed. (London: R. Faulder, 1796; reprint ed.: Westmead, England: Gregg, 1970); Richard Swinburne, *The Concept of Miracle* (New York: Macmillan, 1970); John Earman, "Bayes, Hume, and Miracles," *Faith and Philosophy* 10 (1993): 293-310; George Mavrodes, "Miracles and the Laws of Nature," *Faith and Philosophy* 2 (1985): 333-346; William Alston, "God's Action in the World," in *Divine Nature and Human Language* (Ithaca, N. Y.: Cornell University Press, 1989), pp. 197-222.

[57]Antony Flew in *Did Jesus Rise from the Dead*, ed. Terry L. Miethe (San Francisco: Harper & Row, 1987), p. 4.

[58]John Hick, Introduction, in *The Existence of God*, ed. with an Introduction by John Hick, Problems of Philosophy Series (New York: Macmillan Publishing Co., 1964), pp. 13-14.

[59]William Alston, "Religious Diversity and Perceptual Knowledge of God," *Faith and Philosophy* 5 (1988): 433-448.

[60]Alvin Plantinga, "Two Dozen (or so) Theistic Arguments," Lecture presented at the 33rd Annual Philosophy Conference, Wheaton College, Wheaton, Illinois, October 23-25, 1986.

SUGGESTED FURTHER READING

Craig, William Lane. *The Son Rises*. Chicago: Moody Press, 1981. A thorough examination in popular form of the historical data pertinent to the resurrection of Jesus of Nazareth.

Davis, Stephen T. *God, Reason, and Theistic Proofs*. Grand Rapids, Mich.: Wm. B. Eerdmans, 1997. An excellent contemporary survey of arguments for God's existence, along with a fine discussion of what constitutes a proof and with a chapter on belief in God without arguments.

Hackett, Stuart C. *The Resurrection of Theism*. 2d ed. Grand Rapids, Mich.: Baker Book House, 1982. A classic defense of a number of theistic arguments; includes an interesting rehabilitation of Kant's theory of knowledge, which the reader interested only in the theistic proofs may skip.

Leslie, John. *Universes*. London: Routledge, 1989. The best contemporary discussion of the fine-tuning of the universe for intelligent life.

Moreland, J P. and Nielsen, Kai. *Does God Exist?* Buffalo: Prometheus, 1993. A debate between two leading philosophers, one a theist and one an atheist, covering a wide variety of arguments; a rare chance to see how the arguments fare under criticism.

Plantinga, Alvin. "Reason and Belief in God." In *Faith and Rationality*, pp. 16-93. Ed. Alvin Plantinga and Nicholas Wolterstorff. Notre Dame, Ind.: University of Notre Dame Press, 1983. Plantinga's widely influential essay arguing for the proper basicality of belief in God.

Truth, vols. 3 and 4: "New Arguments for the Existence of God." Dallas: 1991. This out-of-print collection of outstanding articles by the likes of Alston, Evans, Flew, Leslie, Nielsen, Plantinga, Swinburne, and others is still partly available on-line at www.leaderu.com.

Zacharias, Ravi. *Can Man Live Without God.* Dallas; word, 1994. This book addresses the matter of life's meaninglessness if God does not exist.

PROJECTED BOOKLETS IN THE RZIM
CRITICAL QUESTIONS SERIES

William Craig, *God, Are You There? Five Reasons God Exists and Three Reasons It Makes a Difference* (available)

Paul Copan, *Is Everything Really Relative? Examining the Assumptions of Relativism and the Culture of* Truth *Decay* (available)

Scott Armstrong, *Who's Shaping My Life? Assessing the Media's Influence on Our Culture*

Darrell Bock, *Can I Trust the Bible? Defending the Bible's Reliability* (available January 2001)

David K. Clark and James Beilby, *Why Bother With Truth? Arriving at Knowledge in a Skeptical Society* (available)

Douglas Geivett, *Can a Good God Allow Evil? Making Sense of Suffering*

Klaus Issler, *What Does It Mean To Be Human? Understanding Who We Really Are*

Mark Linville, *Is Everything Permitted? Moral Values in a World without God* (available January 2001)

L. T. Jeyachandran *Does the East Have the Answers? Getting Perspective on Eastern Religion and Philosophy*

Stuart McAllister, *Born to Shop? Exposing the Threat of a Consumer Culture*

Paul K. Moser, *Why Doesn't God Make Himself More Obvious? Understanding the God Who Hides and Seeks 9* (available)

Michael Ramsden, *What's the Point? Finding Meaning and Hope in God*

John Mark Reynolds, *Do the Bible and Science Conflict? Reconciling the Differences*

Ravi Zacharias, *What's So Special About Jesus? Encountering Christ Among the World's Religions*

Keith Pavlischek, *Should God Be Excluded from the Public Square? Undestanding the Role of Faith in the Public Life*

Charles Taliaferro, *Do Texts Have Any Meaning? Recovering Meaning and Truth in Texts*

Paul Chamberlain, *Whose Life is it Anyway? Assessing Physician-Assisted Suicide*

Christopher Wright, *Isn't the God of the Bible Cruel and Vindictive? Understanding Ethical Issues in the Bible*

William Lane Craig, *What Does God Know? Reconciling Divine Foreknowledge and Human Freedom*

Douglas Groothuis, *Lost in Cyberspace? Examining and Overcoming the Dehumanizing Effects of the Computer*

Sam Solomon, *Is Islam the One True Religion? Understanding and Engaging the Muslim Mind.*

If you have further questions or are in need of additional resources, please contact

Ravi Zacharias International Ministries,
4725 Peachtree Corners Circle, Suite 250,
Norcross, Georgia, USA 30092.

Website: www.rzim.org
Phone: 800.448.6766
Fax: 770.729.1729
E-mail: rzim@rzim.org

Regional Offices

Canada office
2476 Argentia Road • Suite 203 Mississauga,
Ontario L5N 6M1 Canada • 905.858.2980

European office
97A St. Aldate's,
Oxford OX1 1BT • United Kingdom • 44.1865.203.951

India office
P.O. Box 7307 • Anna Nagar West Extension,
Chennai 600 101 • India • 91.44.626.8014

RZIM is a ministry founded by Dr. Ravi Zacharias with the goal to reach and challenge those who shape the ideas of a culture with the credibility of the message of Jesus Christ.

If you are interested in obtaining a first-rate philosophical journal written with articles written by leading Christian philosophers, we encourage you to subscribe to *Philosophia Christi*, the journal of the Evangelical Philosophical Society (EPS). Please contact:

Paul Pardi
35706 25th Pl. South
Federal Way, WA 98003
eps8451@epsociety.org

Published by RZIM
Ravi Zacharias International Ministries
4725 Peachtree Corners Circle, Suite 250
Norcross, Georgia 30092
www.rzim.org

Library of Congress Cataloging-in-Publication Data
Craig, William Lane, 1999
God, Are You There? / Five Reasons God Exists and Three Reasons It Makes a Difference
ISBN 1-930107-00-5

1. Apologetics.   2. God-Proof-Controversial Literature.
4. Contemporary Issues   5. Christianity-Philosophy.